Littlest Nutcracker for Easiest Piano Tadpole Edition

Tadpole Editions include Black and White illustrations

Selections from Tchaikovsky's Nutcracker Suite for Beginner and Novice Pianists by SilverTonalities!

- *Arabian Dance*
- *Chinese Dance*
- *Dance of the Reed Flutes*
- *Dance of the Sugar Plum Fairy*
- *March*
- *Miniature Overture*
- *Russian Dance*
- *Waltz of the Flowers*

ISBN-13: 978-1975877187

ISBN-10: 1975877187

Images © GraphicsFactory.com

Cover Art © MyClipArtStore.com

Arabian Dance
The Nutcracker Suite

Peter Ilyich Tchaikovsky 1840 - 1893

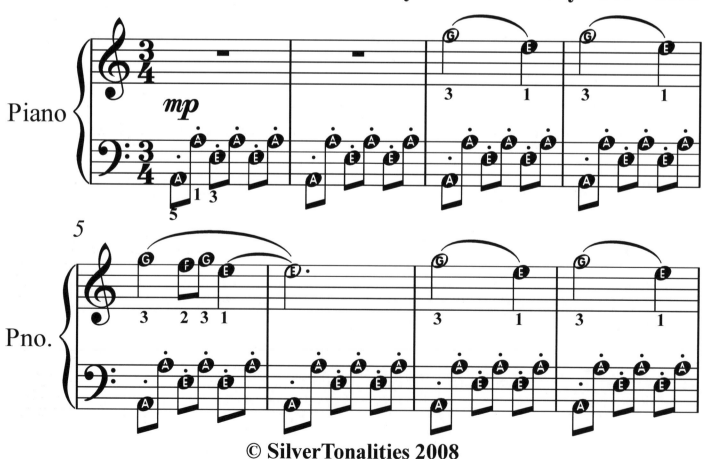

Chinese Dance
The Nutcracker Suite

Peter Ilyich Tchaikovsky 1840 - 1893

Dance of the Reed Flutes
The Nutcracker Suite

Peter Ilyich Tchaikovsky 1840 - 1893

Dance of the Sugar Plum Fairy

The Nutcracker Suite

Peter Ilyich Tchaikovsky 1840 - 1893

March
The Nutcracker Suite

Peter Ilyich Tchaikovsky 1840 - 1893

Miniature Overture
The Nutcracker Suite

Peter Ilyich Tchaikovsky 1840 - 1893

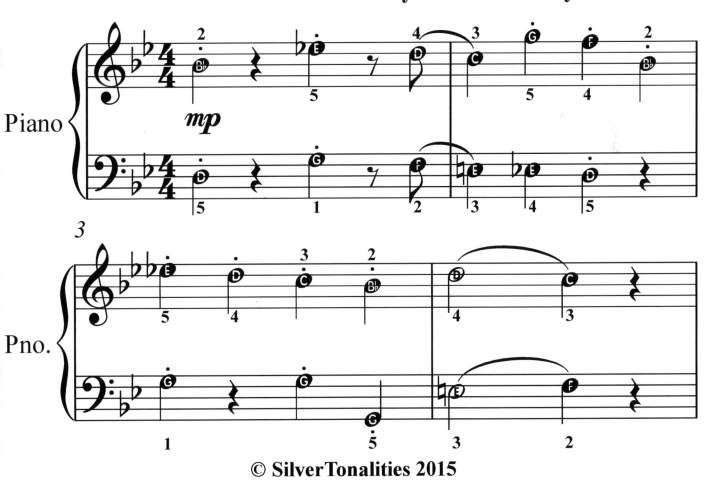

Russian Dance

The Nutcracker Suite

Peter Ilyich Tchaikovsky 1840 - 1893

Waltz of the Flowers
The Nutcracker Suite

Peter Ilyich Tchaikovsky 1840 - 1893

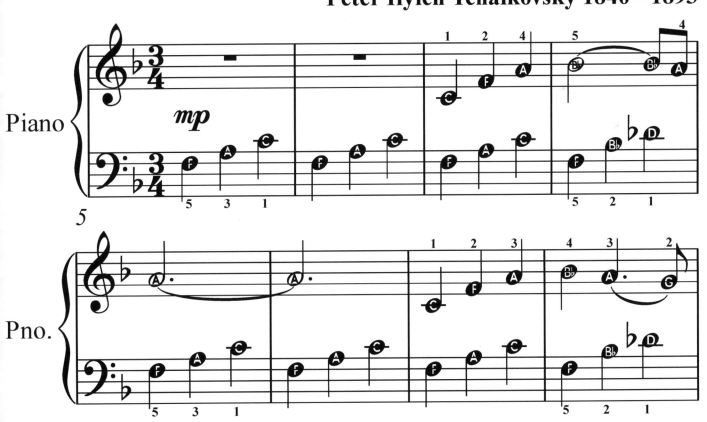

Made in the USA
Lexington, KY
01 November 2017